THE BRITISH

THE BRITISH ARMY BEFORE 1914

The British Army that disembarked in France in August 1914 was, compared to the large French and German armies, a small but highly professional force. Great Britain was at its zenith as a colonial power and its empire stretched across the globe. Because of this, the emphasis was placed on a large navy capable of protecting the Empire's trade routes and the Army was, therefore, of a size required to protect Britain's colonial interests.

Many lessons had been learnt from colonial wars, notably the Boer War of 1899-1902 where the need for a more practical and less visible uniform had become apparent. This led to the adoption of a khaki-coloured service dress and cap in 1902 as well as, in 1908, a modern set of cotton webbing equipment designed to carry all that an infantryman required in the field.

Another important change was made in 1908 when Richard Haldane, the Secretary of State for War, who foresaw a future European war, implemented a series of reforms for the British Army. One of the most important reforms concerned the creation of an expeditionary force (BEF) comprising of six infantry divisions and one cavalry division that would be able to intervene rapidly in the event of a European conflict. Great Britain had, in 1904, signed a series of bi-lateral agreements with France which became

✦ The Territorial Force Imperial Service Badge was awarded to men willing to serve overseas in defence of the Empire. It was worn above the right-hand breast pocket.

known as the Entente Cordiale. Initially this did not mean that Great Britain would intervene to help France in the event of war but in 1911, the Agadir Crisis, involving the French and Germans, led to Franco-British meetings that resulted in Great Britain agreeing to deploy an expeditionary force in France should a conflict with Germany arise. This was not a binding agreement and no formal military alliance was made.

Haldane was also the man behind the creation of the Territorial Force, a reserve force of volunteers who signed up to be called to the colours in the event of war, but only for home defence. This 1908 reform would play an important role in Britain's future war effort. The Territorial soldier had to attend his local drill hall on a regular basis and take part in an annual camp. He was not obligated to serve overseas but could do so on a voluntary basis.

The Territorial Force was, like the Regular Army, based on local recruitment with county battalions. In 1914, it comprised of fourteen infantry battalions and fourteen mounted yeomanry brigades.

✦ Territorials of the Queen's Westminster Rifles at their summer camp in 1913.

FROM MONS TO YPRES

The men of the British Expeditionary Force suffered terribly as they retreated along the sun-parched roads of northern France

The crisis that led to war began on 28 June 1914 with the assassination in Sarajevo of Archduke Franz Ferdinand, the heir to the Austro-Hungarian Empire. Events came to a head at the end of July and rapidly escalated with Germany declaring war on Russia on 1 August, then France on 3 August. Great Britain was bound by the 1839 Treaty of London to protect the neutrality of Belgium. When Germany invaded the latter, Britain too mobilised its Army and declared war on Germany on 4 August, although its navy had already been mobilised on the 1st.

Regiments were called from their various garrison areas and reservists called up. The British Expeditionary Force began embarking for France on 10 August with four infantry divisions and one cavalry, with one infantry division remaining at home in order to deal with any eventual civil unrest. The BEF was commanded by Sir John French and, by 20 August, had assembled at its concentration point near Maubeuge.

The first battle for the BEF came along the Condé canal at Mons, in Belgium, on 23 August. The British held a twenty mile stretch of the canal and fought off a much superior German force. The French, having suffered grievous losses around Charleroi, including 27,000 men killed the previous day, began to pull back, thus leaving the BEF dangerously exposed on both flanks.

The BEF was ordered by Sir John French to begin a withdrawal. With the French and British forces forced back by the German armies as they executed their Schlieffen Plan, the exhausted men fell back along the dusty roads under a sweltering August sun. Constantly pressed by the advancing Germans, the BEF fought rear-guard actions at Le Cateau on 26 August and, in the days that followed, at Etreux, Villers Cotterêts involving the 4th (Guards) Brigade and at Néry where the 1st Cavalry Brigade held off an attack by an entire German cavalry division.

The retreat ended with the French counter-attack on the Marne which began on 6 September. The BEF's commander, Sir John French did not initially wish to take part in the coming battle ; his resolve had been shaken by the retreat and he preferred to pull the BEF back in order to rest and refit. It was only after a personal visit from the new Secretary of State for War, Lord Kitchener, and a request from the French commander Joffre, that Sir John French consented to take part in the advance. The Battle of the Marne ended with the Germans pulling back to positions along the river Aisne. Entrenched positions were now making their appearance and the BEF made several costly attempts to break through the German positions on the high ground along the Chemin des Dames.

However, the BEF was far from the Channel ports that were so vital for its lines of communication and supply and a move north was therefore ordered. This coincided with a series of actions by both sides as they sought to outflank their respective enemies and the BEF fought in a series of bloody actions, notably at La Bassée in October. As the fighting headed further north, the British made an ill-judged decision to land a force at Antwerp and eventually the fighting descended towards the Belgian town of Ypres. It was here that the French, Belgian and British forces held off a series of ferocious German attacks that, if they had succeeded, would have pushed the extremely depleted BEF back to the channel. The Territorials first saw action during the First Battle of Ypres, with the London Scottish suffering heavy losses at Messines.

All that was left now was for both sides to dig in. Trenches now stretched from the North Sea to the Swiss border.

1914
1915
1916
1917
1918

British troops crossing the English Channel on a troopship.

This rare photo shows British soldiers digging the first trenches in the La Bassée sector October 1914. The frontline would remain static here until April 1918.

THE CALL TO ARMS
KITCHENER'S ARMIES

✦ The steely gaze of Lord Kitchener imploring men to do their duty and enlist.

✦ Men rush to join up in 1914.

The British Army consisted of volunteer recruits, unlike the French and German armies who relied heavily on conscription.

Lord Kitchener, who became Secretary of State for War in August 1914, was one of the rare men to predict a long conflict with Germany. He in fact stated that it would take three years and require millions of men. This was an incredible statement at a time when most were saying that the war would be over by Christmas. He therefore began a process of recruiting enough men to sustain the war effort.

The idea of forming 'Pals' battalions of volunteer recruits drew heavily on civic pride, with towns and cities vying to raise as many battalions as possible. In Birmingham, the Daily Post newspaper backed the idea of raising volunteer units and on 28 August, advertised for men to register their names at the newspaper's offices. Three days later there were 1,200 names and within a week, more than 4,500, thus allowing the formation of three battalions which

became the 14th, 15th and 16th Royal Warwick Such was the rush to join up, due to peer pressure the newspapers, civic pride or a sense of adventure that by the end of the year 1,186,357 men ha volunteered. A blind eye was turned to underag recruits or those who would have previously faile to be allowed into the Army due to physical defect These units would now have to be trained an equipped. They would not begin arriving in Franc and Belgium until mid-1915.

✦ 1915 recruitment posters. The streets and buses of Great Britain were adorned with a multitude of posters, making it difficult for men to ignore the call to arms.

THE CHRISTMAS TRUCE

With trench lines now firmly established, the British soldiers settled down to the harsh realities of living in the winter climate of northern France and Belgium. Christmas, the time when back in the hot summer days most people expected the war to be over, was approaching. Both sides had suffered appalling losses, the BEF had lost many of its professional and experienced men and the French had suffered almost a million casualties.

Fighting continued into December for the BEF with a poorly-planned attack launched at Wytschaete on 14 December, ending in failure and heavy losses, with the dead remaining in no man's land. Christmas Eve saw the men in the trenches listening to their enemies singing carols and the next day, in various places along the frontline, truces were held for Christmas Day and beyond. There are many myths surrounding the Truce, notably that of football matches being played in no man's land. The reality is somewhat different. There is no doubt that men exchanged souvenirs or shared a smoke, took time to give those who had died in recent attacks a decent burial, but there is no evidence in battalion war diaries of football matches being played ; the only mention of football is in letters written by a man in the 1/6 Cheshires and another in the 1st Norfolks in trenches near Messines.

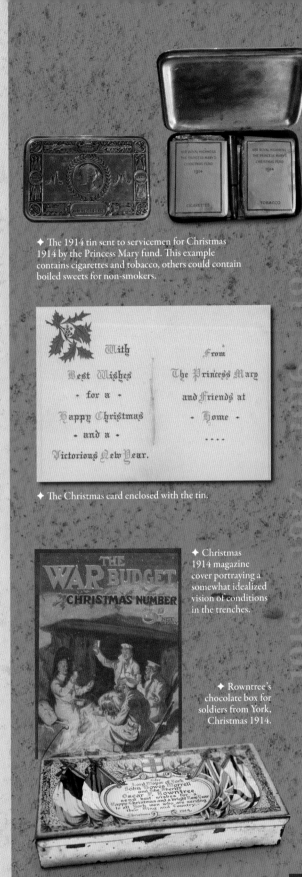

✦ The 1914 tin sent to servicemen for Christmas 1914 by the Princess Mary fund. This example contains cigarettes and tobacco, others could contain boiled sweets for non-smokers.

With Best Wishes - for a - Happy Christmas - and a - Victorious New Year.

From The Princess Mary and Friends at - Home - . . . .

✦ The Christmas card enclosed with the tin.

✦ Christmas 1914 magazine cover portraying a somewhat idealized vision of conditions in the trenches.

✦ Rowntree's chocolate box for soldiers from York, Christmas 1914.

✦ A tin of toffees distributed to the troops by the British Grocer's Federation.

✦ The intrenching tool carrier worn here on the back.

✦ The intrenching tool helve carrier and bayonet frog.

✦ The water bottle.

✦ The cartridge carriers.

PERSONAL EQUIPMENT

The British infantryman disembarking in France in Augu 1914 was equipped with the Pattern 1908 web equipmen This consisted of cartridge carriers capable of holdin 150 rounds of ammunition, a belt, braces, haversac intrenching tool and helve carrier, bayonet frog, wate bottle carrier and pack. The entire set, once assemble could be removed or put on quickly and was, compared other nations' equipment of the time, remarkably moder and comparatively comfortable to wear. British infantr equipment evolved little during the war, indeed the mai modification was ordered in October 1914 for the left-han cartridge carrier due to men complaining of losing round due to the flaps opening.

✦ Private Alfred Griffin, 4th Bn. Middlesex Regt wearing a set of 1908 pattern webbing equipment. He died on 4 May 1917 from wounds sustained during the battle of Arras.

✦ 1914 Pattern infantry equipment.

Due to the inability of the Mills Equipment Company to cope with the heavy demand for new web equipment, a new leather Pattern 1914 equipment was approved at the end of August 1914. It was used to equip the New Army battalions. The two pouches carried 120 rounds. It was unpopular with troops, mainly because it showed they were New Army and not Regular, but also due to its being less comfortable than the 1908 Pattern web equipment.

✦ A soldier of the 10th Service Bn Essex Regt (Forest Gate) wearing 1914 Pattern equipment

CALLING ON THE EMPIRE

On the outbreak of war Britain's dominions rallied around the mother country. Canada, Australia, New-Zealand and South Africa all raised units and dispatched them for overseas service.

Colonies such as India were also called upon to play a role in the war. Indian troops arrived in Marseilles on 30 September 1914 and took part in the fighting at La Bassée in October 1914 and would also see action in the Artois in 1915 as well as a cavalry action on the Somme in 1916.

✦ An Australian Imperial Force badge and Anzac A found on the Bullecourt battlefield.

Canadian troops arrived in Britain in October 1914 and France in February 1915. They played a vital role in halting the German advance at Ypres following the latter's use of chlorine gas on 22 April 1915. The Canadian divisions suffered terrible casualties in the fighting around Courcelette on the Somme in 1916 but went on to achieve one of the war's greatest feats of arms when they took Vimy Ridge in April 1917, then Hill 70 at Loos in July 1917 and the final battles of the war and the victorious advance of the last 100 days.

The call to arms was taken up by other Dominions of the Empire ; South Africa raised an infantry brigade that won fame during its brave stand in Delville Wood on the Somme where its national memorial now stands.

Australia raised 5 infantry divisions that saw combat and the first contingents arrived in France in 1916 following the ill-fated Gallipoli campaign, seeing action in Fromelles in July 1916 then at Pozières on the Somme where they suffered approximately 24,000 casualties. After spending the winter on the Somme front, the Australians went on to fight in the Battle of Arras, Messines and Passchendaele. The final year of the war saw them fight a legendary action at Villers-Bretonneux where they halted the German advance on the vital rail-hub of Amiens. They then went on to play a vital role in the Battle of Amiens in August 1918 and the final advance.

New Zealand fielded one infantry division, seeing action on the Somme, Messines and the 3rd battle of Ypres in 1917. They also played an important role in stemming the German advance across the Somme in March 1918 and in the storming of the fortified town of Le Quesnoy on 4 November 1918.

✦ Indian troops halt in Limoges on their way to the frontline in the autumn of 1914.

✦ A New Zealand NZ dispatch rider.

ARTOIS AND FLANDERS

By early 1915, it was obvious that the war was going to be a long and costly affair. The trenches of the Western Front stretched for over 700 kilometres and the late attacks of 1914 had shown just how difficult it was to attack entrenched positions. With the build-up of the New Army battalions ongoing, the Regular Army found itself involved in bloody battles throughout the year.

The first of these battles was at Neuve Chapelle in France, 10-13 March, and was preceded by an artillery barrage the density of which had not been previously seen, but although the enemy lines were broken, the attack failed due to a lack of reserve troops.

The Second Battle of Ypres began on 22 April with the Germans using chlorine gas for the first time on the Western Front. French colonial troops bore the brunt of this new weapon and the battle developed into a series of actions as the Germans attempted to press home their initial success. The Germans used gas again at Hill 60 in the Ypres salient and the Allies occupied lines closer to Ypres when the battle came to a close in late May.

As the junior partner in the Franco-British alliance, the British were often forced to take part in offensive action at the behest of the French, still commanded by Joffre. On 10 May, and in support of French attacks in the Artois, the British attacked Aubers Ridge which achieved nothing but 11,000 casualties. A further attack was launched at nearby Festubert on 25 May and once again ended up with little material gain at the cost of further heavy casualties.

The middle of the year also saw the arrival of the first New Army battalions, for example, units of the 17th (Northern) Division began arriving in France in July 1915 and settled down into learning how to adapt to the conditions imposed by trench warfare. By the end of the year, most of the New Army divisions were present on the Western Front.

25 September 1915 saw the first large-scale British offensive, once again at the behest of the French as part of and in support of their Artois and

✦ 1st Scots Guards in Big Willie trench, Loos, October 1915. Note the Mills bombs to the right.

Champagne offensives, this time in the mining area of Loos in northern France. This day also saw the British use gas for the first time, although the prevailing weather conditions meant that much of it drifted back into the British trenches. Once again, this attack, involving 6 divisions on the first day, ended in failure due to a lack of available reserves to consolidate initial gains. The battle continued until 14 October. It saw New Army divisions in offensive action for the first time, many only just having arrived in France and resulted in 60,000 British casualties, including 6 generals killed in action.

✦ An early 1915 recruitment poster predicting victory for that year. It was not to be.

GAS

The Germans were the first to gas on the Western Front near Ypres on 22 April 1915. The men who bore the brunt of this terrifying new form of warfare had no form of protection and were forced to use makeshift masks that were, initially, no more than gauze fixed with tape and soaked in urine and accompanied by goggles. The first attempt at supplying troops with anti-gas protection saw the adoption of the Hypo Helmet in June 1915. This consisted of a hood with a mica eyepiece and dipped in chemicals designed to neutralise the effects of the gas. This underwent several modifications and by 1916 the infantry were equipped with the PH gas helmet which consisted once again of a flannel hood with two glass eyepieces and a valve through which to breathe out. A more advanced mask was introduced on the Western Front in the latter part of 1916 and remained in service until the end of the war. This was the Small Box Respirator consisting of a rubberised fabric mask attached via a tube to a metal canister containing chemical absorbent ingredients.

✦ These goggles were initially used by dispatch riders but were used to protect the eyes from chlorine gas until the arrival of the anti-gas hood.

✦ Spicer anti-gas goggles introduced in August 1915.

✦ Sponge anti-gas goggles made with the same eyepieces as the PH helmet.

✦ A soldier of the 28th Bn. London Rgt. (Artist's Rifles) posing with the Small Box Respirator.

✦ 1918 dated gas alert rattle.

✦ The Small Box Respirator with its canvas carrying bag, worn at chest height in the alert position, and its maintenance kit.

✦ The PH helmet introduced in October 1915 and which remained in service throughout 1916 and also into 1917. PH signifies the chemical with which it was impregnated in order to neutralise the gas: Phenate Hexamine.

THE SHRAPNEL HELMET

Fighting conditions in the trenches saw the need arise for an efficient form of protection against head wounds caused by overhead shrapnel. The French adopted a helmet in the spring of 1915 and were followed by the British the same year and finally the Germans in early 1916.

The British helmet was designed by John Brodie and the first helmet to see service in 1915 was called the Brodie's Steel Helmet, War Office Pattern.

The helmet's bowl shape was designed to protect the wearer's head and shoulders from overhead shrapnel. The interior of the steel crown was equipped with an American cloth liner and rubber shock absorbers.

The 1915-designed helmet was modified in 1916 with the MkI. Changes included a new two-part liner and a metal rim to the edge as the latter had been deemed too sharp. The chinstrap was also modified. In order to reduce reflection, sand or sawdust was added to the khaki paint. A further modification was made in 1917 with the addition of a rubber ring placed between the liner and the crown.

✦ The 1905 Pattern Service Dress Cap. This was the cap which the BEF of 1914 wore upon arriving in France.

✦ The soft cap was adopted in autumn 1916 and designed in such a way as to be easily folded and stored.

✦ Helmet, steel, MkI. Note the addition of a rim to the edge of the helmet.

✦ Note the rougher non-reflective paint, achieved by adding sawdust or sand.

✦ A 1915 Brodie's Steel Helmet, War Office Pattern shrapnel helmet with a mottled paint scheme suggested by Brodie of light green, orange and blue patches.

✦ The Winter Service Dress Cap (Gor Blimey) was introduced in November-December 1914. Designed to face the rigours of winter, it was equipped with flaps to protect the ears and neck. It is worn here by Private George Hodgkinson, 1st Bn. Cheshire Rgt. He also wears the 1914-15 economy pattern tunic. He was killed in action at Ypres on 6 May 1915.

✦ A refurbished War Office Pattern shell with hand-painted Signaller's insignia.

✦ The helmet was introduced to prevent wounds from projectiles such as these shrapnel balls which were released from shells exploding over the trenches.

THE YEAR OF THE SOMME

1916 marked a turning point for the British on the Western Front. Douglas Haig was now commander in chief, having replaced Field Marshal French in December 1915. An Allied conference had decided on a series of offensives in the coming year that would at last break the stalemate imposed by trench warfare. For the British, this would take place on the Somme, an area they had taken over from the French in the summer of 1915 as more troops became available with the arrival of the New Army divisions.

The German attack at Verdun in February 1916 upset Allied plans and, as the French were drawn into the horrific attritional battle, it soon became apparent that the main effort for the offensive on the Somme would fall to the British. Haig was not keen on launching his offensive there as it could achieve little strategic gain. He preferred an attack at Ypres where at least a successful offensive could be used to push up the coast and capture ports essential to the German war effort as well as vital rail hubs further inland.

However, the French, still commanded by Joffre, requested that the attack be made on the Somme at the junction with their own armies and where they could keep a close eye on their allies.

The build-up of the New Army divisions meant that the British Army now had 43 infantry divisions and five cavalry on the Western Front. However, many had not yet seen offensive action and had been used for trench holding. As the Verdun battle raged on, the original French contribution to the attack decreased and the coming offensive would now be a question of reducing the pressure on the French at Verdun.

The artillery preparation began on 24 June and saturated the German trenches along a 14-mile stretch of frontline between Gommecourt in the north and Maricourt in the south where the junction was made with the French army near the river Somme. Mines were also dug by specialist tunneller companies deep below no man's land, ready to blow as the attack began.

✦ The Franco-British offensive on the Somme showed the need for a single command. The French and British generals were rarely in agreement when it came to conducting operations. On 1st July, Lt.Col. Fairfax of the 17th Kings Liverpool regiment and Commandant Petit of the French 153rd Infantry Regiment, advanced arm in arm towards the German lines near Maricourt.

The chalk geology of the Somme leant itself to tunnels but this also meant that the Germans could dig deep dugouts. These proved to be impervious to all but the heaviest guns, of which the British did not have enough, instead having a majority of smaller calibre field guns that fired shrapnel in the hope of destroying the belts of barbed wire in front of the German trenches.

Delayed by rainy weather, the attack finally went in at 7.30 am on July 1st. Preceded by a hurricane bombardment of artillery and trench mortars, the men, of whom a great many were the volunteers of 1914 and 1915, left their trenches and began to advance towards the German lines. In most areas, the barbed wire was mostly intact and the Germans, in their deep dugouts, had survived the misery of a week's bombardment. Their Maxim machine-guns were soon in action and began the grisly task of mowing down the lines of advancing men. The losses were staggering ; indeed it would be the blackest day in British military history with casualties of 57,470 including 19,250 men killed.

North of the Albert-Bapaume, the attack was a total failure, except for a small portion of the German frontline south of Thiepval. However, near the junction with the French army, two divisions had broken through and this would shape the strategy for future operations.

ARTILLERY

The British artillery bombardment prior to the attack on the Somme was unprecedented but still insufficient. Lessons had been learnt since the attack at Neuve Chapelle in March 1915 where artillery with the correct level of concentration had played an essential role in destroying the German frontline positions. However, this attack expended around 30% of the 1st Army's field gun shell supplies and this lack of ammunition was attributed to the suspension of the attack. This would have far-reaching repercussions, leading to the Shell Crisis which contributed to bringing down the Liberal government led by Asquith who was thus forced to create a coalition government with Lloyd George appointed as minister of munitions.

Lloyd George saw that the economy would have to undergo changes to meet the demands of the war effort. Improvements were made and more artillery guns produced. However, by 1 July the British did not have enough heavy guns and howitzers essential for destroying defences that the Germans had had two years to strengthen.

Lessons were learned at great cost to the British infantry. The night attack along the Bazentin Ridge on 14 July showed that concentrated heavy artillery, combined with the element of a surprise hurricane bombardment, could subdue a determined enemy defence. Another artillery innovation that saw use on the Somme was that of the "creeping" barrage, literally a curtain of shell fire that gradually lifted towards the enemy trenches and behind which the infantry could advance with the aim of being on top of the enemy before the latter could emerge and set up their machine-guns.

Other artillery innovations were flash spotting and range finding. The Somme had shown that attacking troops were extremely vulnerable to enemy counter-barrages. Enemy artillery was positioned out of sight, behind ridges or hills. Prior to flash spotting and range finding, a target was spotted by balloon

✦ Royal Field Artillery men with 1902 pattern bandoleers for carrying fifty rounds of rifle ammunition.

✦ The 18-pounder shell was the mainstay of British artillery in the Great War.

1914

1915

1916

1918

observation or by aircraft. Ranging shots were then fired, observed and corrected until the target was neutralised, a process that was slow and led to expending precious ammunition. A Canadian artillery officer, Captain Harold Hemming, came up with a method of observing enemy artillery flashes and using triangulation to identify the exact positions of the guns.

Sound ranging also used triangulation to locate enemy artillery positions. Listening posts along the line were equipped with microphones and oscillographs that recorded the strength and direction of sound waves. The time intervals between listening posts were recorded and then triangulation was used to calculate the exact location of the gun. These techniques were used with great success before the Arras offensive in April 1917.

In 1914, British artillery was organised within divisions. As the war progressed and the need for massed artillery became apparent, fifty percent of the divisional field artillery was removed in 1916 and placed under Army or Corps command and therefore more easily moved to where they were needed. There were also heavy artillery and siege batteries and these played an increasingly important role as the war evolved.

✦ Shell carrier jacke
for transporting fou
13 or 18 Pounder sh

✦ 18 Pounder field gun in action
at St. Leger, August 1916.

THE BATTLE OF THE SOMME
JULY TO NOVEMBER 1916

The terrible losses of the first day did not lead to a suspension of the offensive, on the contrary ; if the pressure was to be taken off the French at Verdun, the British would have to press the enemy in order to force the latter to send reserves to the Somme sector.
A series of piecemeal attacks saw the British being drawn into costly fighting, especially around Thiepval and further south where gains had been made on the first day.

The next major attack took place at the early hours of 14 July, a perilous night-time attack that the French allies had described as an attack organised for amateurs by amateurs. The attack was launched at 3.25 am with four infantry divisions and was preceded by a hurricane artillery bombardment lasting for only five minutes but with a concentration of 950 guns for an attack frontage of 5.5 kilometres. The attack was a success and the British reached the village of Longueval and High Wood which dominated the next ridge line.

The battle once again settled into attrition. Reserves were slow to move forward and exploit the gains made and the short window of opportunity where a real breakthrough might have been achieved. A cavalry charge was even made near High Wood but ended in failure. Over the next two months the fighting for High Wood and Delville Wood reached unheard of levels of ferocity and the casualty list grew ever longer with losses of 13,000 around High Wood and similar losses at the nearby Delville Wood. German reserves were being drawn into the battle however and they too suffered horrendous losses under the Franco-British attacks.

15 September saw another large-scale attack being made, this time with a new invention, the tank. The nine-division attack captured the German held villages of Courcelette, Martinpuich and Flers and High Wood and Delville Wood were captured at last. Of the 49 tanks called into the battle, only 32 reached their allocated start positions with a further seven breaking down, thus only leaving 25 capable of going forward with the troops. These lumbering landships provided little tactical advantage, used as they were in small groups, but they did strike fear into the German defenders and nine were success-ful in penetrating the German lines. Losses again were high for the Canadian, New Zealand and British attackers with casualties of over 29,000 in one day.

With the capture of Pozières, Courcelette and Martinpuich, the German held fortress of Thiepval on the high ground above the Ancre valley was now ready to be assaulted frontally and from the flank and rear. The attack started on 26 September and forced the German defenders from the remains of the village and up to the infamous Schwaben Redoubt which overlooked the German lines north of the Ancre towards Beaumont Hamel. The focus of the Somme fighting was now north of the Albert-Bapaume road with a further British attack along the Ancre Valley and Beaumont Hamel in November. In the southern sector, the British line stalled along the Guedecourt ridge. The battle was officially halted on 18 November 1916. Losses on all sides were appalling ; the British Empire losses were 420,000 and around 200,000 for the French. The Germans lost in the region of half a million men. Territorial gains were slender but the battle had achieved its aim of drawing the German reserves away from Verdun. It had also dealt a grievous blow to the German army in terms of experienced manpower. The British Army had suffered terrible casualties but the New Army battalions had gained precious battle experience.

May you-
rush through
all opposition
in 1916

GRENADES

The pre-war British Army had been trained to a very high degree in musketry, something which was put to deadly use in the initial war of movement before the trench lines were established.

Trench warfare, however, soon highlighted the need for grenades, an essential weapon for clearing trenches and dugouts in an attack.

✦ The Nº23 Mills Bomb was designed to be used as a rifle and hand grenade. In its rifle grenade configuration, a rod was screwed into the base plug. A steel cradle attached to the muzzle of the rifle held the lever in place until the grenade was discharged using a special round.

The British entered the war sparsely equipped with the expensive No 1 Grenade. Adopted in 1908, it had a long wooden throwing handle with a cloth streamer designed to make the grenade hit the ground nose first, thus detonating the impact fuse. It soon proved cumbersome in the trenches and despite variants with shorter handles being made, production was halted in 1915 and stop-gap grenades were made by using old tins filled with ammonal and scrap metal.

1915 also saw the introduction of the Mills Bomb, a grenade that would see service in various forms up to the 1980s. It was issued in May 1915 but did not see wide use until mass production allowed it to be generally issued in 1916. Throughout the war, three versions of this grenade were made, the Nº5, Nº23 and the Nº36.

✦ Men of the 2nd Battalion Argyll and Sutherland Highlandersat Bois Grenier in 1915. Note the jam tin bombs and Hales grenades.

The Bomber's Greeting
IV Corps 1915

✦ The N°1 Grenade Mk 3 with shorter handle. The design was based on Japanese grenades studied during the Russo-Japanese war. It soon proved unsuitable for trench warfare.

✦ Martin Hale rifle grenade introduced in 1915. Rifle grenades played an important role in trench warfare and were a constant nuisance and source of daily casualties on both sides.

✦ The Mills Bomb was adopted in 1915. It was designed by William Mills based on a pre-war design by a Belgian officer. It became the standard British Army grenade. A good thrower could launch the grenade 15 metres with the fragmented body capable of creating a danger area of up to 60 metres.

✦ The Hales N°2 Mk 2 introduced in 1915 but soon phased out with the arrival of the Mills Bomb.

✦ The Battye Grenade was a stop gap design and the first attempt to manufacture a bomb suited for trench warfare. It was made in Béthune in France and consisted of a cast iron cylinder filled with ammonal and closed with a wooden plug and Nobel igniters.

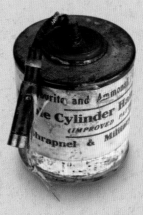

✦ The Jam Tin bomb is perhaps the most famous of all the stop gap measures used by the British Army in 1915. They were filled with scrap metal and gun cotton then equipped with a simple ignition fuse.

✦ A 1915 dated N°5 Grenade crate. Note the circular tin containing the detonators that were added when the grenades were issued to the men.

THE BATTLES OF 1917 : ARRAS, YPRES, CAMBRAI

During the terrible winter of 1916-17 the German army on the Somme sector pulled back to the pre-made positions of the Hindenburg Line, leaving a trail of devastation in their wake.

Plans had been made for a series of Franco-British offensives. The French, commanded by Nivelle, would launch a series of attacks on the Aisne against the German held heights of the Chemin des Dames whilst the British would attack a week earlier in the Artois, thus drawing away German reserves.

Following a week-long artillery barrage, the British and Canadians attacked in the Arras sector on 9 April. The initial success was stunning compared with previous battles. One of the greatest feats of arms was the Canadian Corps capture of the strongly held Vimy Ridge. Using flash spotting and sound ranging techniques, the German artillery was mostly neutralised. However, the offensive once again ground to a halt as the Germans rallied.

Further attacks were made against the Hindenburg Line at Bullecourt by British and Australian troops with the latter suffering horrendous casualties. The Battle of Arras achieved little, especially as the French attack launched on 17 April was a total disaster. The offensive was halted on 16 May and the daily casualty figures were even higher than the Somme with average daily losses of 4,076.

The British Army had barely time to catch its breath before the next offensive was undertaken. The Messines ridge on the southern sector of the Ypres salient had been in German hands since October 1914. Tunnelling companies had been busy since 1916 digging deep under the lines in order to place 21 mines* beneath the German trenches and strongpoints. At 3.10 a.m. on 7 June, the mines were blown simultaneously, literally blowing the Germans off the ridge in a series of explosions that were heard and even felt in England and which killed an estimated 10,000 enemy troops.

The British and Anzac troops swept forward protected by a creeping barrage and captured this vital high ground. The fighting on the ridge went on for another week before operations were halted.

The next phase of the offensive took place on 31 July against the Ypres salient. The strategic aim was to push the Germans back from Ypres then roll up their positions along the coast, thus capturing German held ports used for their U-Boat operations that were crippling the British war effort and causing massive food shortages at home.

The 3rd Battle of Ypres has gone down in history as a byword for the futility and heavy losses of the Great War. The battle gradually pushed the enemy back in a series of offensive operations before grinding to a halt in November in the muddy wasteland of the Passchendaele ridge where the Australians and Canadians suffered terrible casualties for little gain.

Further south in France, plans were afoot for yet another offensive, this time near Cambrai and a mere ten days since the end of the offensive in Flanders and this time involving the first ever massed tank attack with 437 tanks and six infantry divisions. Initial gains were spectacular, up to five miles in places and to such an extent that church bells were rung in celebration back in Britain. However, the battle soon settled down into the familiar pattern of attrition and the Germans launched a huge counter-attack on 30 November, eventually capturing all the ground they had lost and even taking previously held British positions.

*Two failed to explode, possibly due to flooding in the tunnels. One detonated in 1955 during a thunder storm, the other lies beneath a re-built farm !

✦ British wounded at a casualty clearing station in Blangy during the battle of Arras. The average daily loss rate during the two-month offensive was 4,072 killed, wounded, missing and taken prisoner.

THE TUNNELLERS

Underground warfare for the British began as early as December 1914 when the Germans blew up mines under British trenches at Givenchy. It was now urgent to create units capable of undertaking this type of warfare.

Before the war, John-Norton Griffiths's civil engineering company was working on sewage systems in Liverpool and Manchester. In December 1914 he had written to the War Office offering his services and expertise in tunnelling.

Following the German mine attack, he was summoned to see Kitchener and was soon authorized to form tunnelling companies under the authority of the Royal Engineers. The British Army went on to form 26 Royal Engineer Tunnelling Companies, and the New-Zealanders, Australians and Canadians also formed their own.

These units played an essential role in the war, as seen at Messines, but also made safe dugouts to shelter men from the shelling, one of the most impressive shelters, made by the New Zealand tunnellers, can be visited today at Arras.

✦ Norton-Griffiths served in the Boer War. He became an MP in 1910 and was, before the war, at the head of a successful civil engineering business.

✦ British 1915 dated shovel and 1914 dated pick.

✦ The Lochnagar crater at La Boisselle, Somme. The tunnel for the mine was started in November 1915 by the 185th Tunnelling Company, but was taken over and completed by the 179th Tunnelling Company who took over in March 1916.

✦ The mine craters at Bois Français, Somme, 1915.

1914

1915

1916

1917

1918

TRENCH RAIDS

Trench raiding became a regular and dreaded feature of trench warfare. Men in static positions could soon lose their offensive spirit and both sides could easily lapse into a live and let live attitude. The first trench raids were often small affairs aimed at achieving moral ascendency over the enemy, causing havoc or capturing prisoners in order to find out what units were on the other side of No Man's Land and their state of morale. Many raids were amateur affairs that led to more casualties for the British than the enemy. However, by the end of the war they could involve a great amount of planning, preparation and manpower. A good example of this is the 50th Brigade (17th Northern Division) two-battalion trench raid at Beaumont Hamel in May 1918 in which they killed over 150 enemy and brought back thirty prisoners.

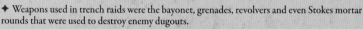

✦ A raiding party of the 1/8th (Irish) King's Liverpool Regiment, 55th Division, at Wailly, France. Photograph taken the morning after a night raid 17/18th April 1916.

✦ Weapons used in trench raids were the bayonet, grenades, revolvers and even Stokes mortar rounds that were used to destroy enemy dugouts.

✦ Webley flare guns and flares. These were used along the frontline at night to see if there was any enemy activity in no man's land or to call down artillery along the S.O.S. Line, or to call back trench raids.

1914 1915 1916 1917 1918

THE BRITISH OFFICER

The pre-war British Regular Army officer was invariably of upper class origin and had a public school background. However, as the war progressed and losses mounted, especially among junior officers, men from other social backgrounds gained commissions or were promoted from the ranks.

The infantry officer was given an allowance to purchase his uniform and equipment. The uniforms were of superior quality to the other ranks but also made them conspicuous in an attack or to enemy snipers. The early officer's tunic bore the rank insignia on the cuff but, from 1916 onwards, a less visible rank insignia was worn on the shoulder straps. Other ranks' uniforms were also worn to make an officer become less of an obvious target in an attack.

✦ Mk VI Webley service revolver.

✦ Officer's cap to an ASC officer.

✦ Regulation issue compass.

✦ Cloth insignia indicating a Machine Gun Corps ammunition supply column.

✦ Books such as this were available to officers in order to learn about conditions in the trenches before they arrived on the Western Front.

✦ Rank was denoted on the cuffs. 1916 saw the introduction of shoulder rank insignia designed to render the officer less conspicuous.

✦ Officer's shrapnel helmet with cover. The insignia is that of the 8th Division Signals Company.

✦ A young infantry subaltern, Dorsetshire Regiment, 1914.

✦ Army Service Corps lieutenant. The ASC were responsible for providing food, equipment and ammunition. They worked in the ports as well as up to the frontline dumps from where the infantry units would then move supplies up to the frontline itself.

1917

FEEDING TOMMY

Feeding the millions of soldiers in the trenches of the Western Front was an incredible task. Rations were transported from the ports to railheads, then by motorised transport to forward dumps from where horse-drawn transportation was used to take them closer to the frontline.

The standard rations comprised of corned beef, Maconochie, a much-despised stew of fatty meat and vegetables, and biscuits so hard they could break teeth. Other rations consisted of bacon, jam, tea and condensed milk. The monotony of this diet could be broken in villages behind the lines where civilians relieved the Tommies of their pay in impromptu cafes called estaminets where the soldiers could buy egg and chips, omelettes and cheap wine or beer.

The Expeditionary Force Canteens were another source of food and sold in bulk or in stores behind the lines to units or individual soldiers. The YMCA and Church Army also provided food and a warm drink to soldiers, often very close to the frontline.

✦ A tin of Fray Bentos corned beef.

✦ Lantern with holder at the top for heating a mug of tea.

✦ Dixie used for cooking rations.

✦ The British infantryman's mess tin.

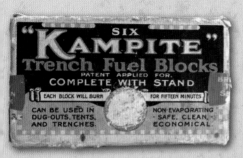

✦ Private purchase trench cookers. Men could also receive food parcels sent from home.

✦ Rum jar. Men could be issued with a spoonful of rum in the morning and evening as well as before going over the top.

✦ Petrol cans were re-used to transport water. The men often complained of water and tea tasting of petrol.

✦ Bully Beef ration crate.

✦ Thermos food container used to transport warm food to frontline troops.

LE *SHORT MAGAZINE LEE-ENFIELD*

✦ The SMLE MkIII* introduced in late 1915. A simplified version of the MkIII.

The SMLE was the standard issue rifle for the British and Commonwealth soldier in the Great War.

The Mk III, introduced in 1907 along with a longer sword bayonet, fired the .303 inch cartridge. Its fast-operating bolt action combined with a ten-round magazine meant that a well-trained infantryman could fire fifteen aimed rounds a minute. Early encounters with British riflemen led the Germans to believe that they were facing machine-gun fire of which only two were issued per battalion at the beginning, whereas in fact they were facing the well-trained British marksmen of a professional army. Other rifles were used, such as early version Lee-Enfields or even Lee Metfords, issued to New Army or Territorial units until stocks of the more modern MkIII became available.

✦ Lee-Enfield rifle mounted with a P.P. Co. telescopic sniper scope.

✦ Lee-Enfield equipped with a grenade launcher cup.

✦ The five-round charger. The magazine had a ten-round capacity.

✦ Wooden rifle ammunition bandolier crate.

✦ The SMLE could be equipped with wire cutters.

✦ A British sniper in 1915.

LIFE BEHIND THE LINES

The British soldier was in close proximity to French and Belgian civilians and sometimes, in the case of the Loos sector in 1915, within a few miles of the trenches. French civilians did a roaring trade with Tommies desperate to break the monotony of army rations. Markets sold all kinds of provisions that could be taken up to the frontline and cafes sold good meals, with the more upmarket establishments being reserved for officers. The Military Police were also at hand to make sure that opening times were respected and to keep an eye on any black market activities such as army issue rum finding its way to civilians !

Bonne et heureuse année!
Les soldats anglais envoient leurs meilleurs voeux à leurs héroïques camarades français.
1 Janvier, 1917.

✦ Guides de conversation franco-anglais d'achat personnel.

The British Army also organised activities for the men at rest behind the lines. After a spell in the trenches, the men would spend a period of training or reorganisation, if following an attack. Divisions had their own concert parties which took the shape of music hall acts popular in Britain at the time, with men dressing up to play any feminine roles.

✦ The Butterfly Follies of the 19th Division.

✦ Concert party programme held by The Crumps at Barastre, Somme, June 1917. They were the 41st Division's concert party troop.

Sport was also an important feature of life behind the lines with inter-battalion football matches, boxing bouts and divisional horse shows.

✦ A battalion football team.

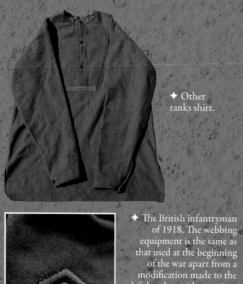

✦ Other ranks shirt.

✦ The British infantryman of 1918. The webbing equipment is the same as that used at the beginning of the war apart from a modification made to the left-hand cartridge carriers.

✦ Introduced by Army Order Nº4 1918, the chevrons denoted overseas service (1915-1918 here). A fifth red chevron denoted overseas service in 1914.

✦ Divisional insignia began to be used in 1918. The white dot and dash symbolize the top of the one and seven.

✦ 1917 dated boots.

THE INFANTRYMAN OF 1918

An infantryman of the 6th Dorsetshire Battalion, 17th (Northern) Division. Having voluntarily enlisted in late 1914 as part of Lord Kitchener's recruitment drive, he arrived in France in July 1915 following a period of basic training. The first few months were spent with spells of acclimatizing to the rigours of trench life in the Ypres salient and the sodden sector of Armentières. The summer of 1916 saw the terrible fighting on the Somme, first at Fricourt then, towards the end of the offensive, the Transloy ridge. 1917 saw the 6th Dorsets in action at Arras, notably in the rubble of the infamous chemical works at Roeux. October saw the Battalion fighting in Langemarck in the Ypres salient. The final year of the war was seen in at Havrincourt, facing the German Hindenburg Line. The enemy offensive of 21 March forced the British back across the former battlefields of the Somme.

After four months of trench warfare the fight back began, for the 6th Dorsets, in August, pushing the enemy out of the ruins of Thiepval.

October saw a determined enemy stand along the river Selle at Neuvilly and it was here that the 6th Dorsets suffered their heaviest casualties of the entire war. The final fighting took place in Mormal forest. In three months of incessant fighting and an advance of seventy miles, the 6th Dorsets had suffered 849 casualties.

✦ Soldier's wash roll.

✦ 1917 dated towel and soap.

1914 1915 1916 1917 **1918**

THE FINAL YEAR — 1918

The offensives of 1917, especially at Ypres, had left the British Army exhausted and weakened. The government, led by Lloyd George, had also sent precious British divisions to Italy in order to shore up the front on the Isonzo following the Italian rout at Caporetto. Added to this was the government's reluctance to send over any further troops to make up for losses and the French demand for the British Army to take over more frontline south of the river Somme. It was at this time that divisions reduced their strength from twelve battalions to nine. All of this made the British Army dangerously exposed to the expected German attack, now that the latter had been able to bring its divisions back from the Eastern Front.

The German hammer-blow fell on 21 March 1918 between south of Arras and the Oise river. The 5th Army, led by General Hubert Gough, was pushed back across the old Somme battlefields, but a stand was finally made and the Germans halted before they could capture the vital rail hub of Amiens. Further German offensives were made, notably in the Armentières region, but again eventually ran out of steam.

The tide was finally turned in a series of counter-attacks, the first, led by the French, pushed the Germans back across the river Aisne. The next attack involved British, Commonwealth and French troops on 8 August. The Amiens offensive was a great success and saw a first-day advance of 11 kilometres. The battle also saw a collapse of German morale and saw thousands of troops surrender, leading the German commander, Erich Ludendorff, to call it the black day of the German army.

Amiens was the start of the Hundred Days Offensive. The Germans were slowly pushed back by the British and Commonwealth troops who now implemented all the lessons acquired from a painful and costly four-year learning process. Troops now advanced in platoon-sized groups, using fire and movement techniques, supported by tanks, artillery and aircraft. By the time the war finally came to an end on 11 November, the British Army had become a formidable and modern fighting machine.

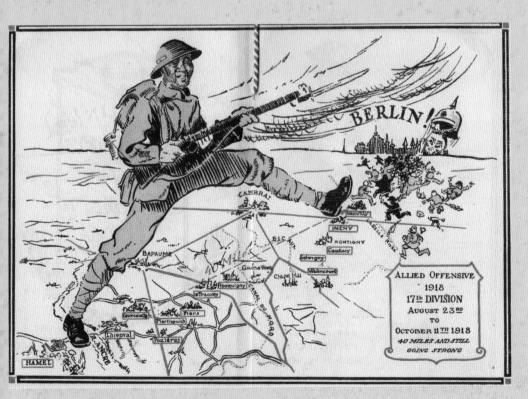

✦ 17th Division card showing advancing soldier during the Hundred Days Offensive.

THE SCOTTISH SOLDIER

The Scottish Highlander soldier of 1914 was one of the most visually striking. When it came to his uniform, the Scottish soldier differed from his English, Welsh and Irish counterparts. In 1914, the Highlanders wore a kilt in the tartan of his regiment, protected on campaign by a beige-coloured apron, hose-tops, khaki drill spats and the traditional Glengarry headwear. The standard 1902 pattern tunic was often rounded at the front in order to make space for the full-dress sporran. The Glengarry was later replaced for wear in the field by the Tam 'o Shanter.

There were eight Scottish battalions in the 1914 British Expeditionary Force. As the war progressed and the New Army units grew in strength, there would eventually be four Scottish divisions on the Western Front, the 9th (Scottish) Division, 15th (Scottish) Division, 51st (Highland) Division and the 52nd (Lowland) Division. The men of this proud nation produced fine fighting troops and took part in all of the major engagements of the Great War.

✦ *Royal Scots Fusiliers*

✦ *London Scottish Highlanders*

✦ A young soldier of the Seaforth Highlanders, 26 February 1916. Note the Imperial Service Badge and rounded tunic front designed to provide easy access to the sporran.

✦ *Gordon Highlanders*

✦ *Cameronian Scottish Rifles*

✦ Scottish soldier with standard service dress tunic.

✦ *Black Watch*

✦ *Tyneside Scottish*

28

HOME LEAVE

For the average infantryman, the chance to return home and see loved ones came once a year if he was lucky. Officers, who had the added burden of responsibility, tended to enjoy more frequent periods of leave. Once the lucky man had his leave ticket he would begin his journey home, often involving a long drawn-out train journey to one of the Channel ports. A troopship would then transport him back to Blighty where another train journey would eventually take him to his home town. For a man living in or near London, he could go from the trenches to home in a day, for those less fortunate, it could take two days and this was part of his leave time.

For most men, returning home was not always an easy experience; many memoirs relate the growing gulf between the men who had experienced the horrors of the frontline and those at home whose knowledge of the war derived from often rose-tinted newspaper articles.

South Eastern and Chatham Railway.

JULY 1st, 1916,
AND UNTIL FURTHER NOTICE.

THE

RETURN LEAVE TRAINS

WILL LEAVE

Victoria at 7.50 a.m.
(S.E. & C.R.)

DAILY (Sundays included).

Via BOULOGNE, from Platforms Nos. 2 and 3
Via CALAIS, from Platform No. 10

BY ORDER.

✦ A poster announcing changes to trains departing for France. The mainline stations, especially those in London, would have been busy with soldiers returning from, or going to, the Western Front. Canteens were set up as well as bureaux de change. Soldiers were also issued with a leaflet explaining what they were not allowed to bring back into the country, notably dangerous souvenirs. The British rail network played an unsung but vital role in transporting men and materiel to the embarkation ports.

The proximity of France was such that if prevailing weather conditions allowed, the sound of artillery fire could be heard in England. Bernard Adams, author of Nothing of Importance, was convalescing in Kent in the summer of 1916 and could hear the distant rumbling of the guns in France.

✦ A soldier of the Loyal North Lancashire Regiment poses outside his home in full kit before returning to France and Flanders. Note the 1914 Pattern equipment and Lee-Enfield N°1 Mk 1.

H.M. FORCES OVERSEAS (IN UNIFORM).

COMBINED LEAVE AND RAILWAY TICKET.

No. C 244170   Third Class.

FOR ONE PERSON ONLY.

To FRANCE.

✦ The precious leave ticket that meant some respite from frontline service.

✦ Soldiers resting inside the Preston Soldiers and Sailors Buffet, April 1917.
This buffet was run by local women keen to support the war effort.
They provided refreshments and a quiet place to rest for servicemen passing via Preston.

TRENCH EQUIPMENT

The conditions encountered in trench warfare led to the adoption of specific equipment. It was not, of course, safe to look over the trench parapet without exposing oneself to the ever alert enemy snipers. Issue and private purchase periscopes were used to keep an eye on No Man's Land during the daytime. Wire cutters were also issued, not only for use in cutting exits in the British wire prior to an attack, but also for use when repairing or replacing wire defences at night. British frontline dugouts tended to be less well-equipped than their German counterparts which often had electric lighting. Many types of lanterns were issued or privately purchased in order to provide a little light in dugouts and also behind the lines.

✦ A soldier in a sap-head at Cuinchy uses a periscope to look out for any enemy activity.

✦ Issue torch, dated 1918.

✦ Periscope designed for use with the bayonet.

✦ Private purchase Orilux torch named to T. Davis of the Royal Warwickshire Regiment.

THE LIFEGUARD POCKET PERISCOPE
PATENT Nº 163/15
SOLE MAKERS
F. DUERR & SONS
MANCHESTER
S.W.

✦ Private purchase collapsible trench periscope made by Duerr's of Manchester, a jam manufacturer which is still in business today.

✦ 1917 dated trench pump

✦ Wooden 1917 trench periscope.

✦ Folding trench lantern
for use with candles.

✦ Private purchase
trench lantern, the Khaki
Kombination Kandlebox.

✦ Various types of issue wire cutters.

1918

AFTER THE WAR

The British 4th and 2nd Armies entered Germany on 17 November as part of the occupying forces of Rhineland. With the cessation of hostilities came the problem of demobilising the millions of men and women present on the Western Front. Priority was given to men who had worked in key industrial sectors. However, many of these men had been called-up late in the war and this led to the unfair situation of men who had served the longest being the last to return home.

In places such as Calais and Folkestone, this led to serious unrest and mutinies.

✦ A battlefield grave on the Somme in 1916. It is easy to see how the makeshift markers were subsequently lost. The dead of the Great War continue to be found to this day.

Upon leaving his unit, the soldier was given a medical examination then spent time in a transit camp before sailing for home. Upon arrival in Great Britain, he would spend some time in a dispersal centre before being issued with a railway warrant to his home town.

In November 1918, the British Army had just under 4 million men. This number was reduced to 900,000 a year later and by 1922, the Army had just over 230,000 men.

The time had come to look for the missing. Graves had been scattered all across the battlefields and their markers often lost due to the ebb and tide of the fighting. Exhumation Companies remained in France and Flanders and began looking for the bodies of the

fallen. Cemeteries were supervised by the Imperial War Graves Commission and permanent headstones and memorials began to be added in the 1920s.

For the families, travel companies such as Thomas Cook ran trips to the former Western Front for those who could afford it. Others could obtain a photograph of their loved one's grave via the IWGC. A fee was charged to families who wished to have a personal inscription on the headstone.

✦ A British mother visits her son's grave at Oppy Wood in the early nineteen thirties.